INTERMEDIATE
PIANO DUET

ANDREW LLOYD WEBBER'S

1 PIANO, 4 HANDS

The
PHANTOM
of the
OPERA

T0053067

ISBN 978-0-7935-5836-0

HAL•LEONARD®
CORPORATION
7777 W. BLUEMOUND RD. P.O. BOX 13819 MILWAUKEE, WI 53213

THINK OF ME

SECONDO

Music by ANDREW LLOYD WEBBER
Lyrics by CHARLES HART
Additional Lyrics by RICHARD STILGOE

THINK OF ME

PRIMO

Music by ANDREW LLOYD WEBBER
Lyrics by CHARLES HART
Additional Lyrics by RICHARD STILGOE

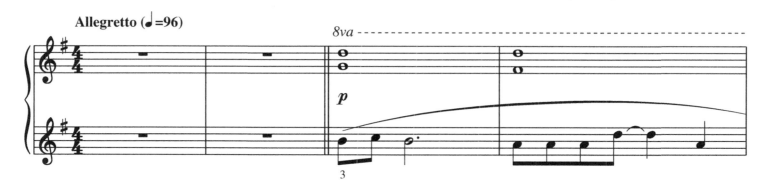

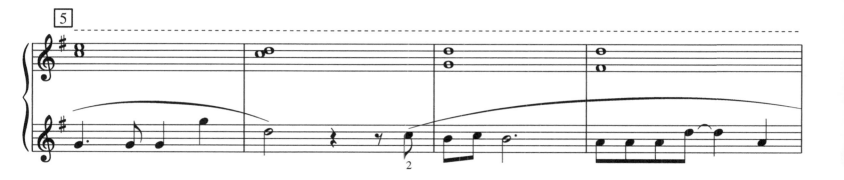

PRIMO

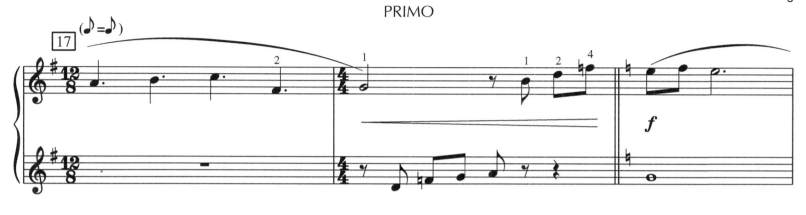

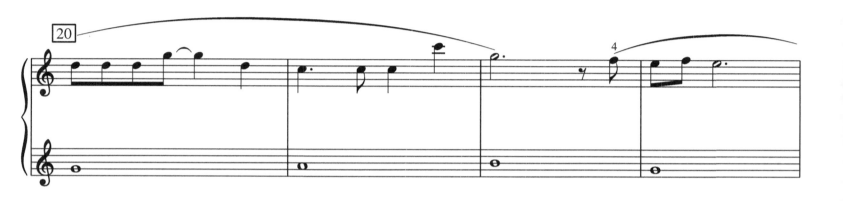

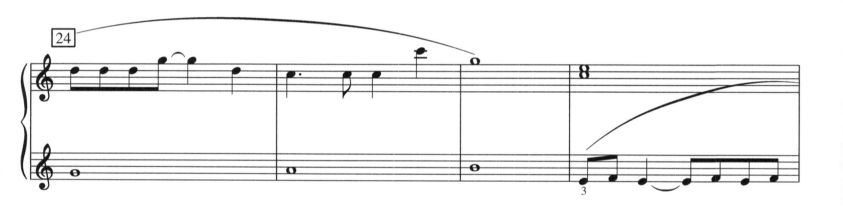

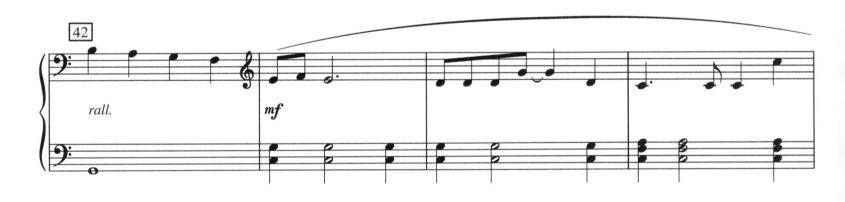

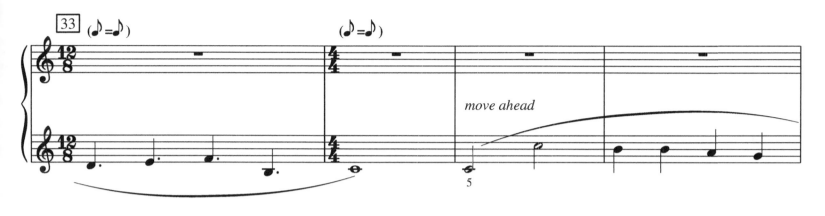

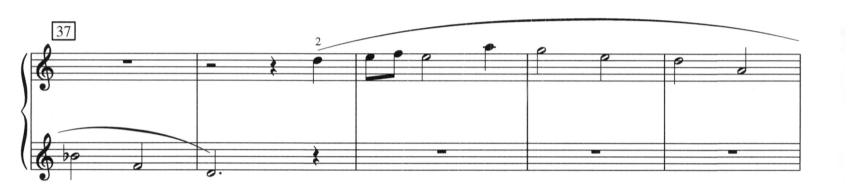

SECONDO

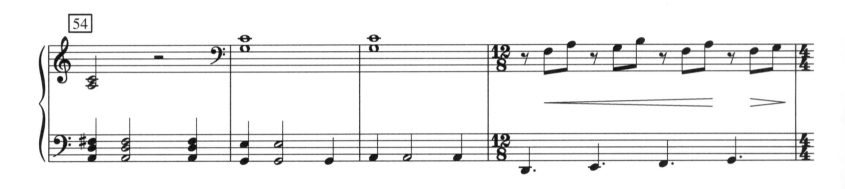

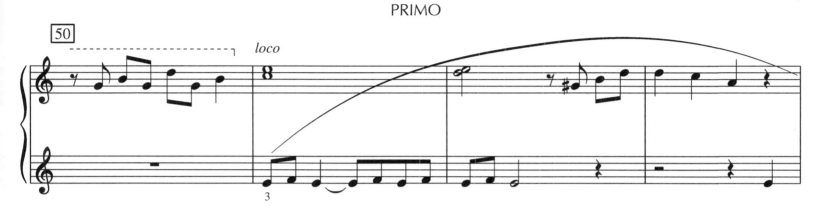

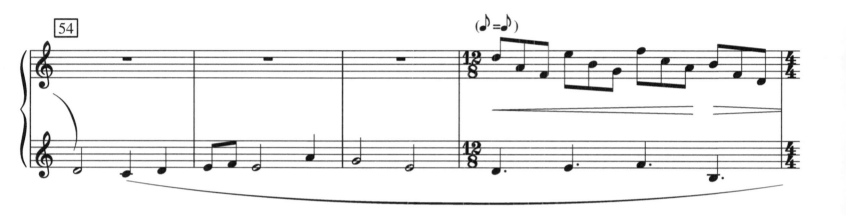

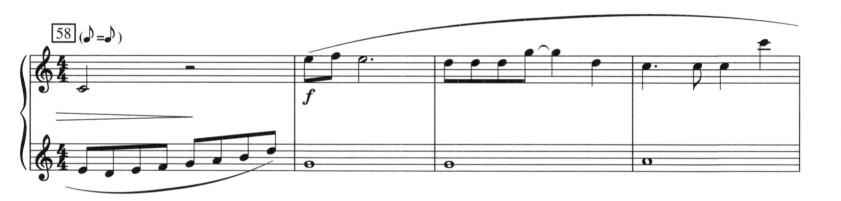

PRIMO

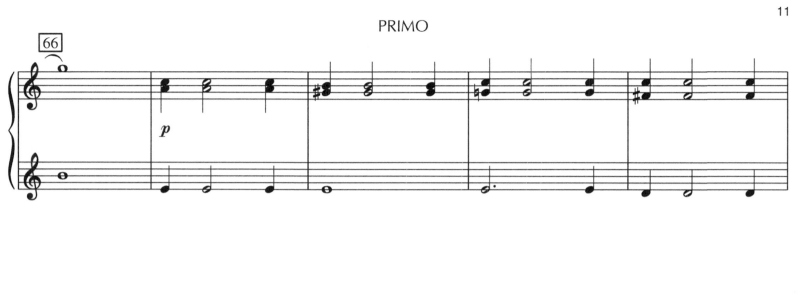

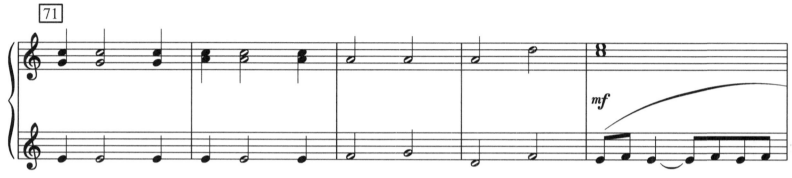

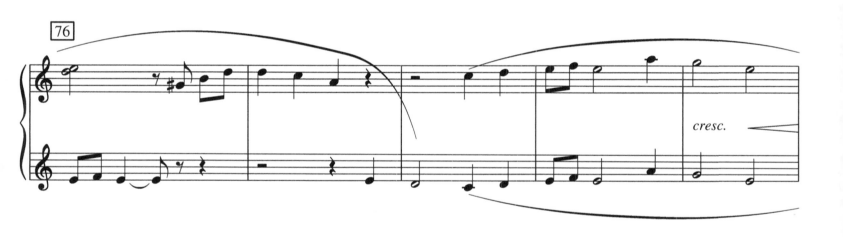

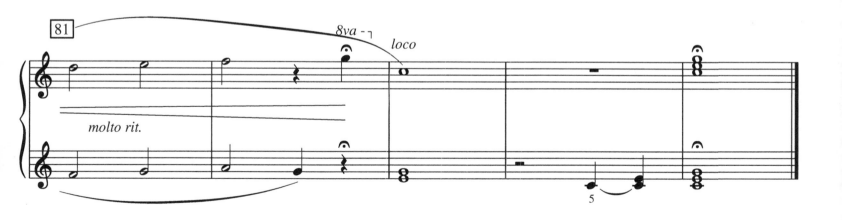

ANGEL OF MUSIC

SECONDO

Music by ANDREW LLOYD WEBBER
Lyrics by CHARLES HART
Additional Lyrics by RICHARD STILGOE

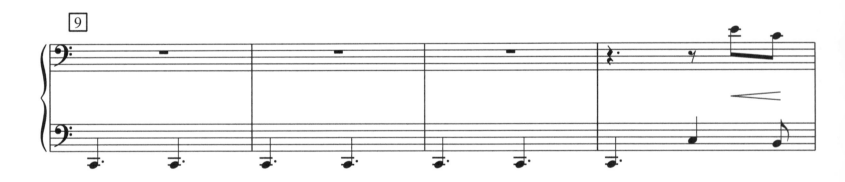

ANGEL OF MUSIC

PRIMO

Music by ANDREW LLOYD WEBBER
Lyrics by CHARLES HART
Additional Lyrics by RICHARD STILGOE

SECONDO

PRIMO

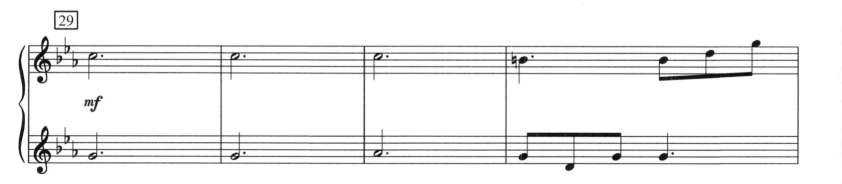

SECONDO

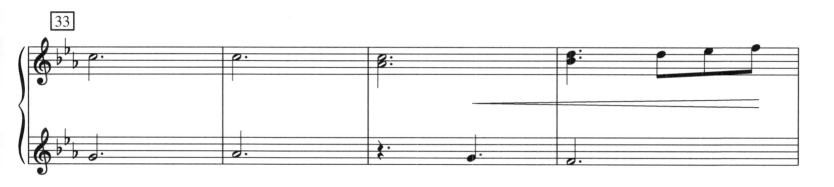

THE PHANTOM OF THE OPERA

SECONDO

Music by ANDREW LLOYD WEBBER
Lyrics by CHARLES HART
Additional Lyrics by RICHARD STILGOE and MIKE BATT

Allegro-Vivace

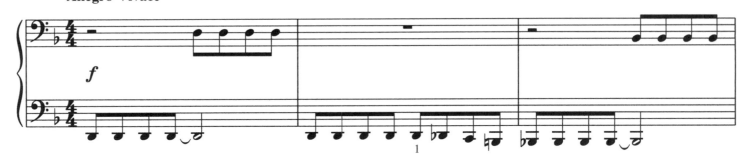

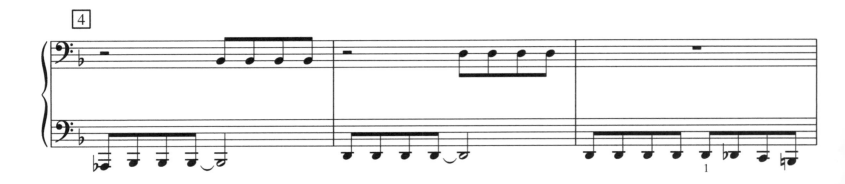

THE PHANTOM OF THE OPERA

PRIMO

Music by ANDREW LLOYD WEBBER
Lyrics by CHARLES HART
Additional Lyrics by RICHARD STILGOE and MIKE BATT

Allegro-Vivace

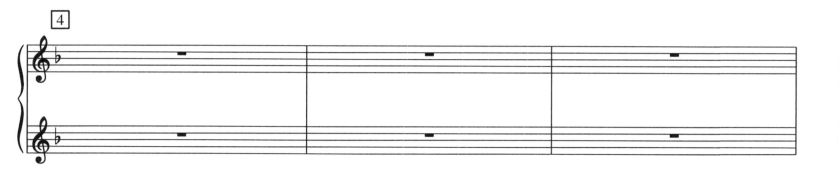

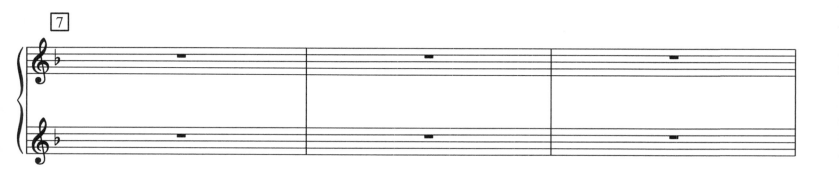

SECONDO

13

16

19

22

PRIMO

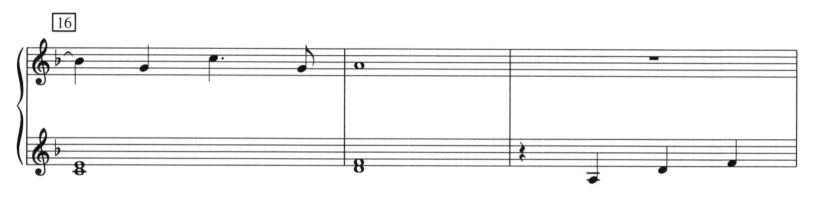

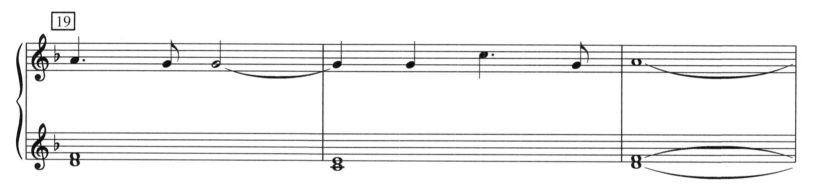

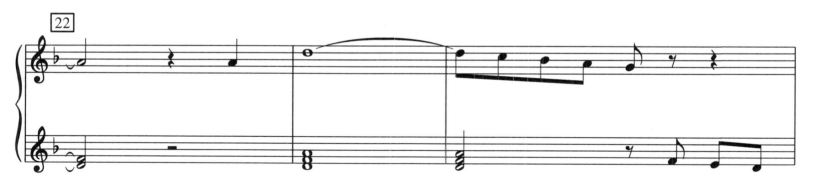

SECONDO

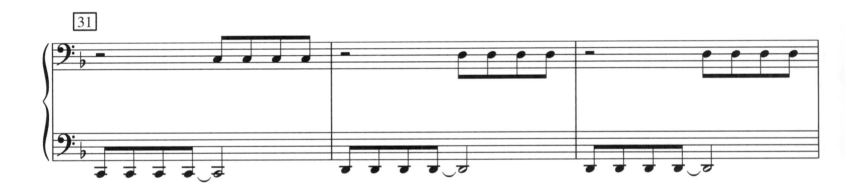

PRIMO

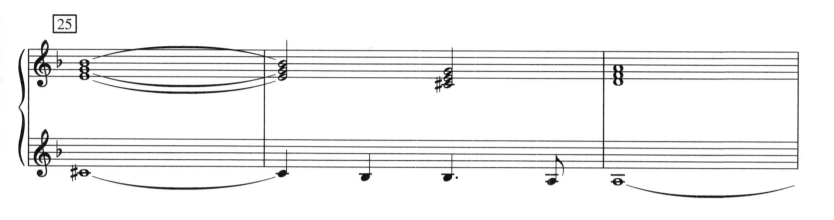

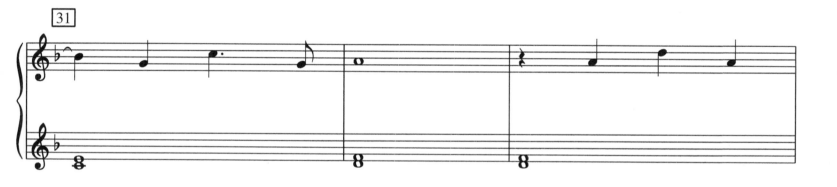

SECONDO

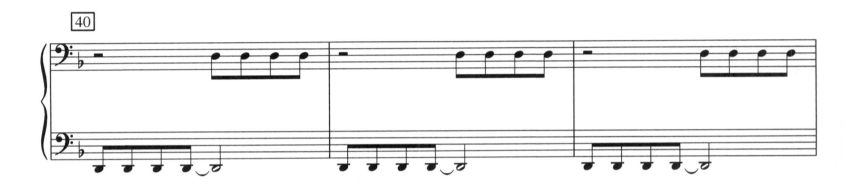

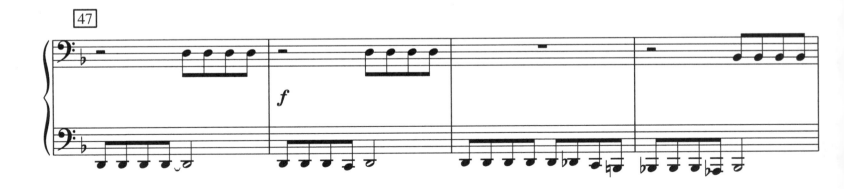

PRIMO

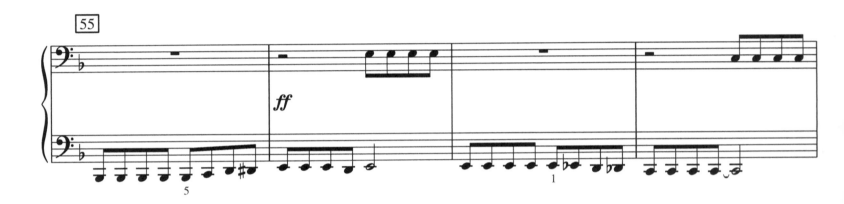

PRIMO

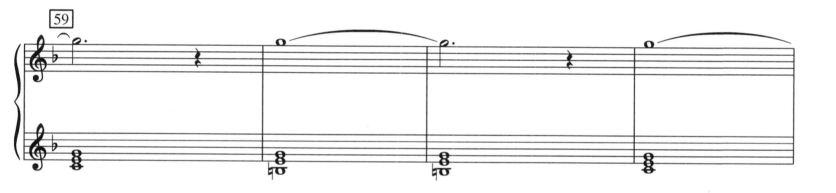

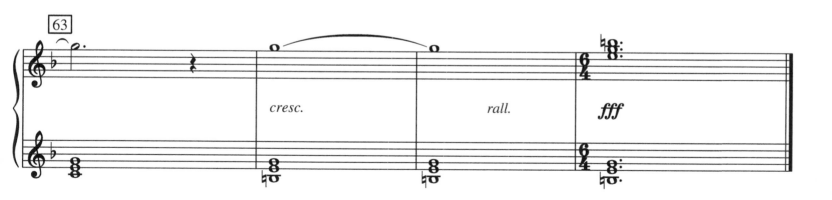

THE MUSIC OF THE NIGHT

SECONDO

Music by ANDREW LLOYD WEBBER
Lyrics by CHARLES HART
Additional Lyrics by RICHARD STILGOE

THE MUSIC OF THE NIGHT

PRIMO

Music by ANDREW LLOYD WEBBER
Lyrics by CHARLES HART
Additional Lyrics by RICHARD STILGOE

SECONDO

PRIMO

SECONDO

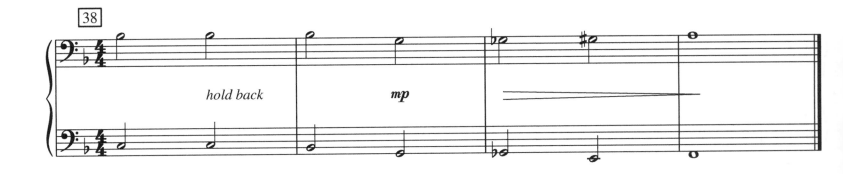

PRIMO

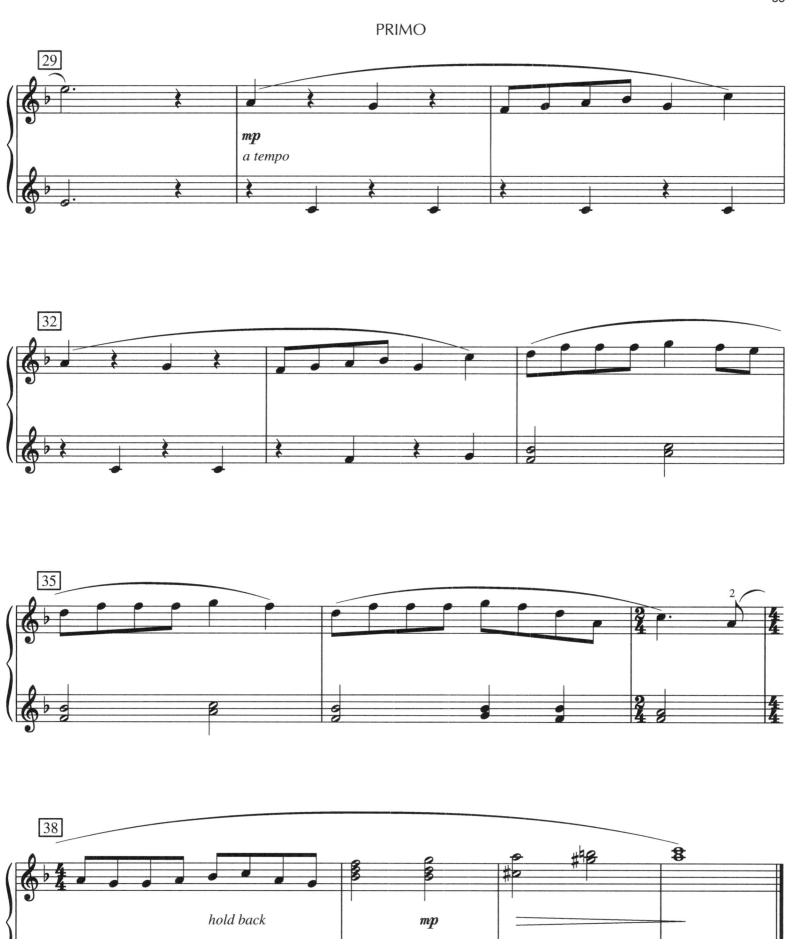

PRIMA DONNA

SECONDO

Music by ANDREW LLOYD WEBBER
Lyrics by CHARLES HART
Additional Lyrics by RICHARD STILGOE

Stately Waltz

PRIMA DONNA

PRIMO

Music by ANDREW LLOYD WEBBER
Lyrics by CHARLES HART
Additional Lyrics by RICHARD STILGOE

Stately Waltz

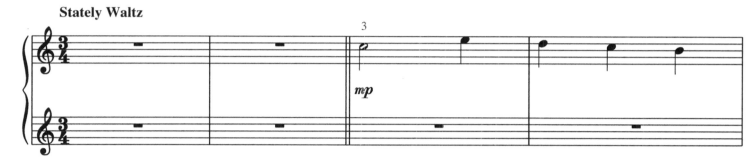

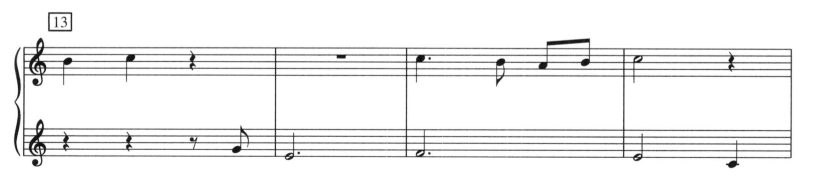

SECONDO

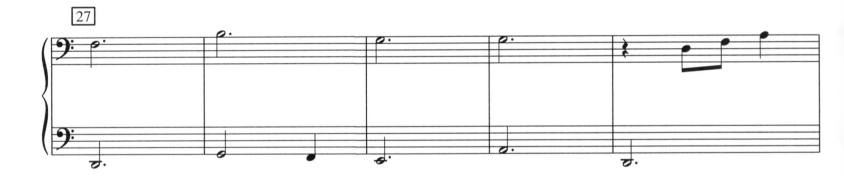

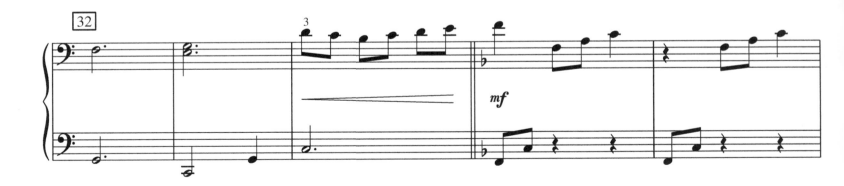

PRIMO

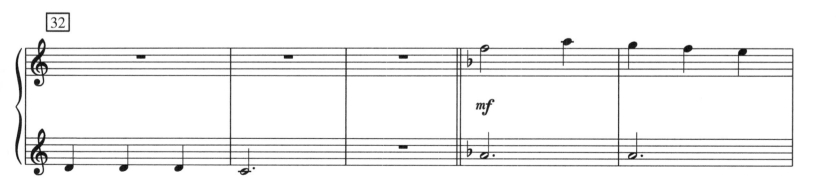

SECONDO

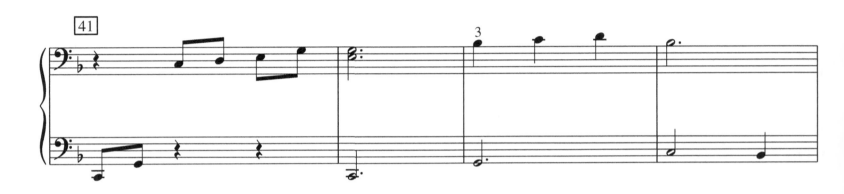

PRIMO

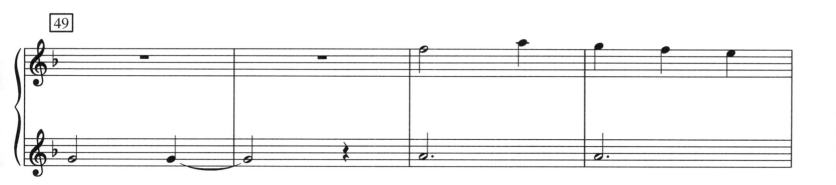

SECONDO

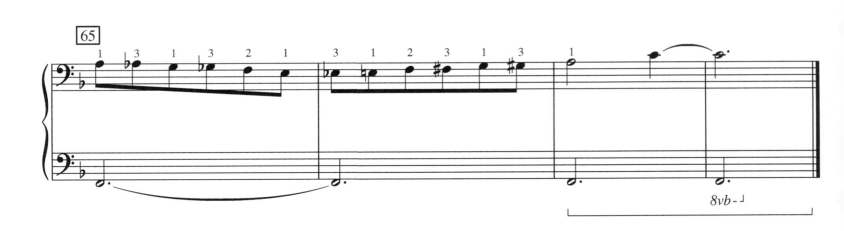

PRIMO

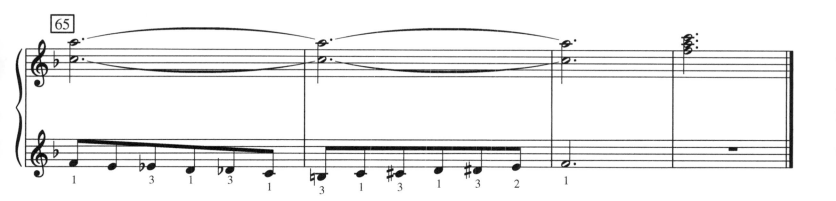

ALL I ASK OF YOU

SECONDO

Music by ANDREW LLOYD WEBBER
Lyrics by CHARLES HART
Additional Lyrics by RICHARD STILGOE

ALL I ASK OF YOU

PRIMO

Music by ANDREW LLOYD WEBBER
Lyrics by CHARLES HART
Additional Lyrics by RICHARD STILGOE

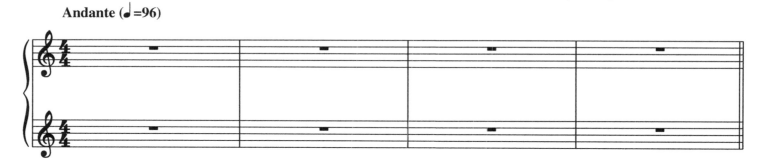

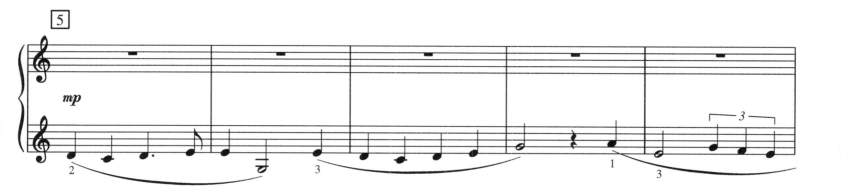

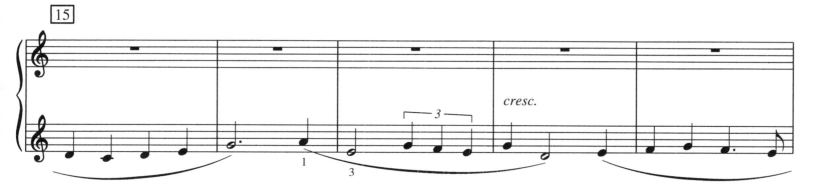

SECONDO

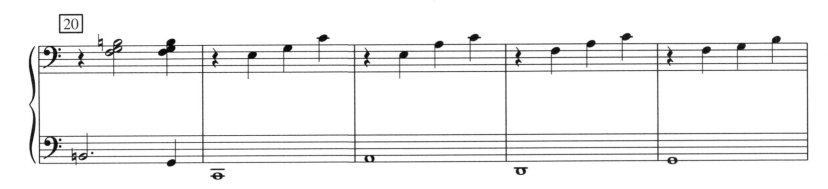

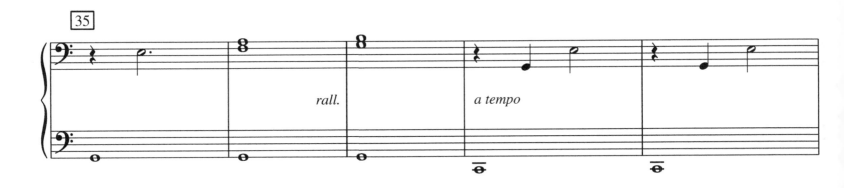

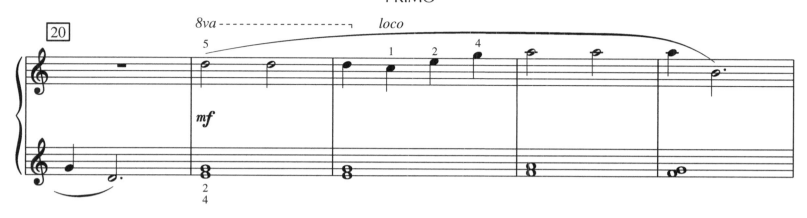

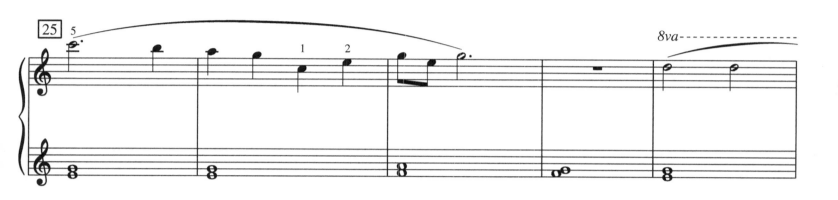

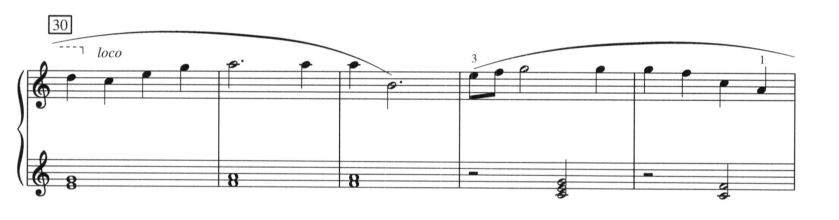

SECONDO

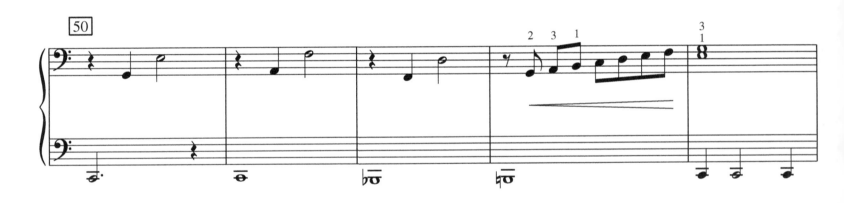

PRIMO

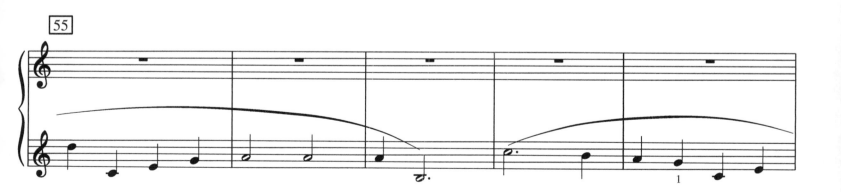

SECONDO

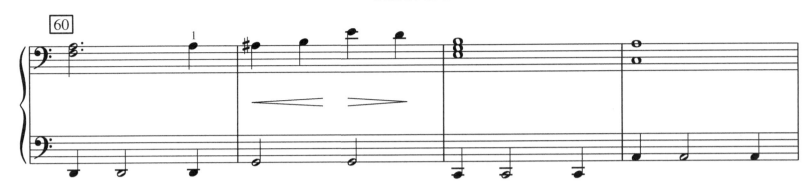

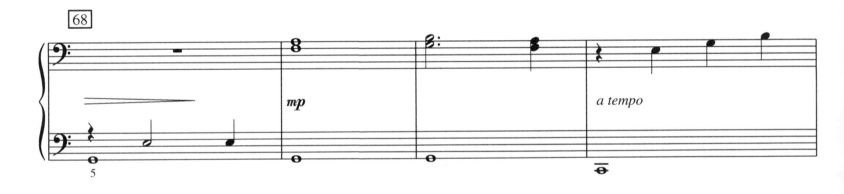

PRIMO

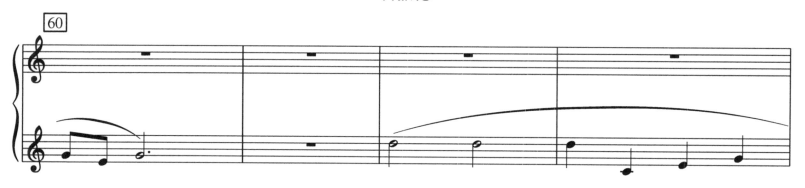

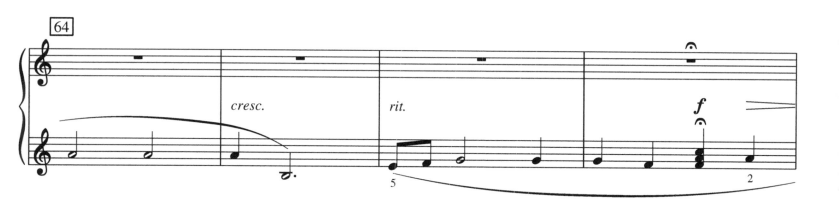

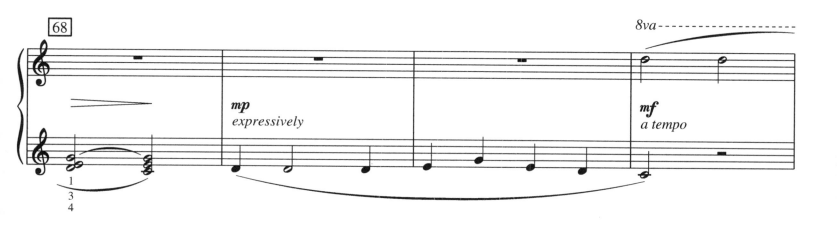

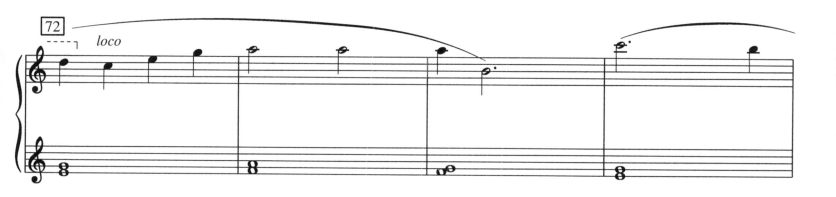

SECONDO

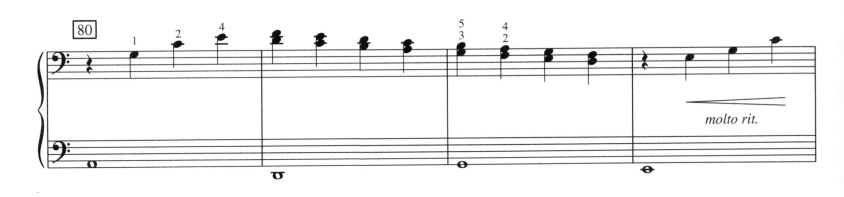

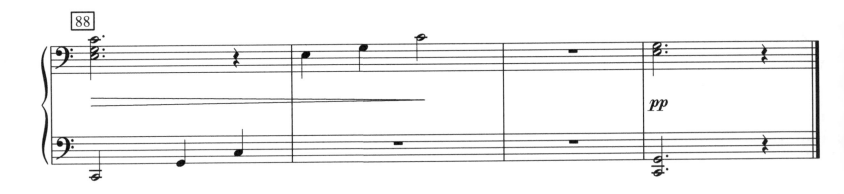

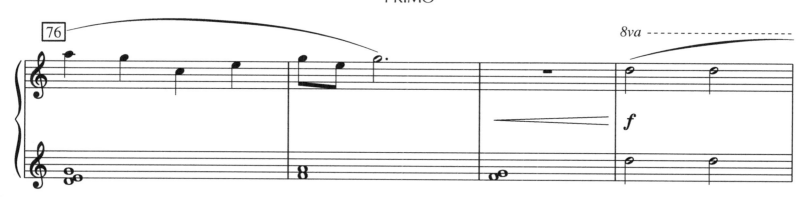

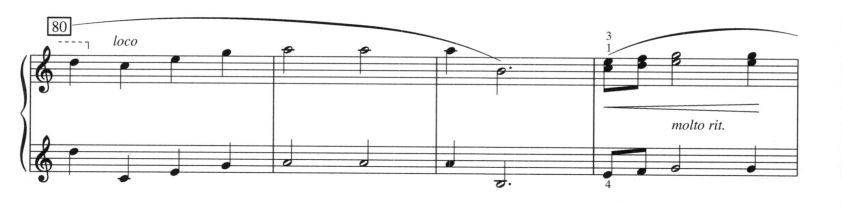

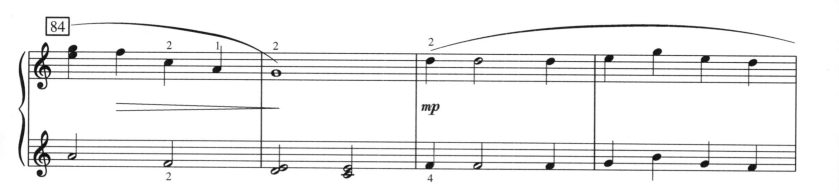

MASQUERADE

SECONDO

Music by ANDREW LLOYD WEBBER
Lyrics by CHARLES HART
Additional Lyrics by RICHARD STILGOE

Lively

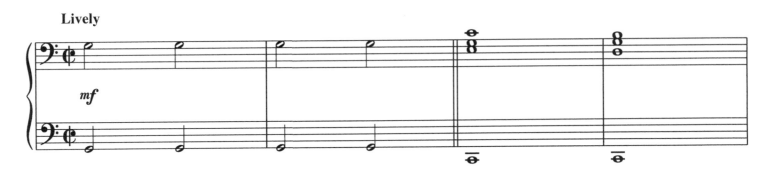

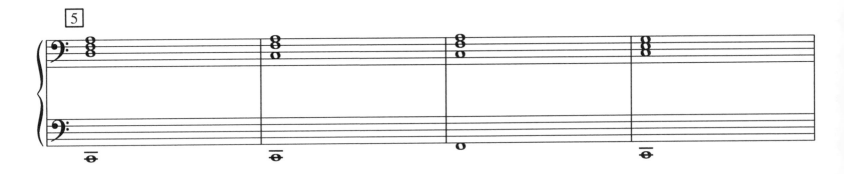

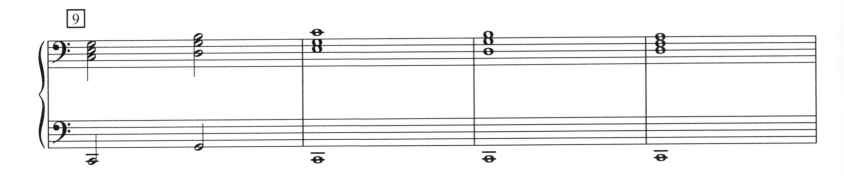

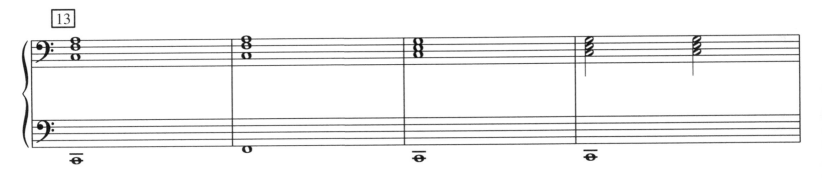

MASQUERADE

PRIMO

Music by ANDREW LLOYD WEBBER
Lyrics by CHARLES HART
Additional Lyrics by RICHARD STILGOE

SECONDO

PRIMO

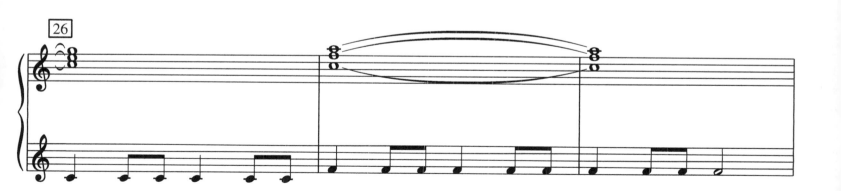

SECONDO

PRIMO

SECONDO

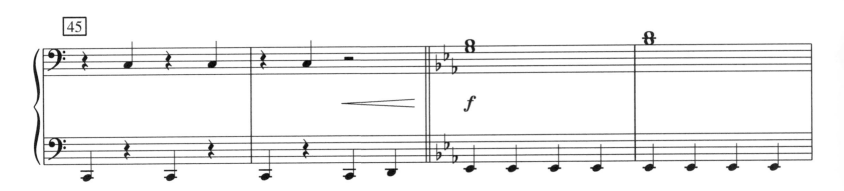

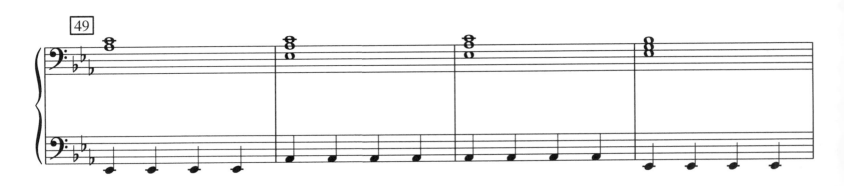

PRIMO

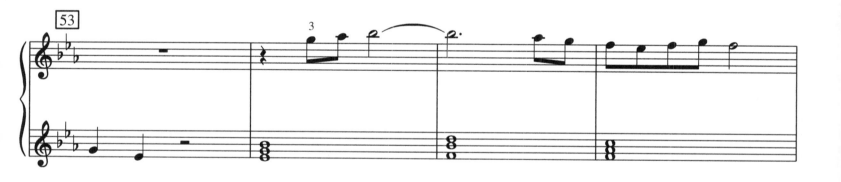

WISHING YOU WERE SOMEHOW HERE AGAIN

SECONDO

Music by ANDREW LLOYD WEBBER
Lyrics by CHARLES HART
Additional Lyrics by RICHARD STILGOE

WISHING YOU WERE SOMEHOW HERE AGAIN

PRIMO

Music by ANDREW LLOYD WEBBER
Lyrics by CHARLES HART
Additional Lyrics by RICHARD STILGOE

SECONDO

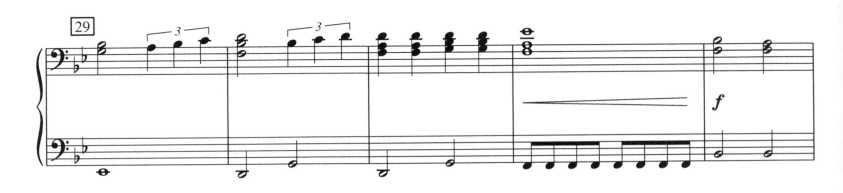

PRIMO

Piano For Two

A VARIETY OF PIANO DUETS FROM HAL LEONARD

LI – THE BEATLES PIANO DUETS – 2ND EDITION

Features 8 arrangements: Can't Buy Me Love • Eleanor Rigby • Hey Jude • Let It Be • Penny Lane • Something • When I'm Sixty-Four • Yesterday.

00290496..$10.95

I – BROADWAY DUETS

9 duet arrangements of Broadway favorites, including: Cabaret • Comedy Tonight • Ol' Man River • One • and more.

00292077 ....$12.99

LI – BROADWAY FAVORITES

A show-stopping collection of 8 songs arranged as piano duets. Includes: I Dreamed a Dream • If Ever I Would Leave You • Memory • People.

00290185 ....$9.95

LI – COLLECTED SACRED CLASSICS

Arranged by Bill Boyd

8 classics for piano duet, including: Ave Maria • A Mighty Fortress • Hallelujah from *Messiah* • and more.

00221009 ....$9.95

I – DISNEY DUETS

8 songs: Candle on the Water • Colors of the Wind • Cruella de Vil • Hakuna Matata • Someday • A Spoonful of Sugar • Winnie the Pooh • Zip-A-Dee-Doo-Dah.

00290484 ....$12.95

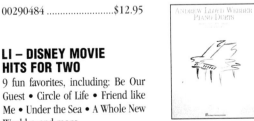

LI – DISNEY MOVIE HITS FOR TWO

9 fun favorites, including: Be Our Guest • Circle of Life • Friend like Me • Under the Sea • A Whole New World • and more.

00292076 ....$14.95

LI – DUET CLASSICS FOR PIANO

8 classical melodies, arranged as piano duets. Includes: Liebestraum (Liszt) • Minuet In G (Beethoven) • Sleeping Beauty Waltz (Tchaikovsky) • and more.

00290172 ....$6.95

LI – GERSHWIN PIANO DUETS

These duet arrangements of 10 Gershwin classics such as "I Got Plenty of Nuttin'," "Summertime," "It Ain't Necessarily So," and "Love Walked In" sound as full and satisfying as the orchestral originals.

00312603..$10.95

I – GREAT MOVIE THEMES

8 movie hits, including: Chariots of Fire • Colors of the Wind • The Entertainer • *Forrest Gump – Main Title* • Theme from *Jurassic Park* • Somewhere in Time • Somewhere, My Love • *Star Trek® – The Motion Picture* • and more.

00290494..$9.95

UI – LOVE DUETS

7 songs: All I Ask of You • Can You Feel the Love Tonight • Can't Help Falling in Love • Here, There, and Everywhere • Unchained Melody • When I Fall in Love • A Whole New World (Aladdin's Theme).

00290485 ....$8.95

LI – ANDREW LLOYD WEBBER PIANO DUETS

arr. Ann Collins

8 easy piano duets, featuring some of Andrew Lloyd Webber's biggest hits such as: All I Ask of You • Don't Cry for Me Argentina • Memory • I Don't Know How to Love Him.

00290332..$12.95

I – MOVIE DUETS

9 songs, including: Chariots of Fire • *The Godfather* (Love Theme) • *Romeo and Juliet* (Love Theme) • Theme from *Schindler's List* • and more.

00292078 ....$9.95

UI – COLE PORTER PIANO DUETS

What a better way to play these 6 Cole Porter love songs such as "Do I Love You?" "I Love Paris," "In The Still of the Night," than with a partner?

00312680............................$9.95

UI – ROCK 'N' ROLL – PIANO DUETS

Ten early rock classics, including: Blue Suede Shoes • Don't Be Cruel • Rock Around the Clock • Shake, Rattle and Roll.

00290171............................$9.95

I – THE SOUND OF MUSIC

9 songs, including: Do-Re-Mi • Edelweiss • My Favorite Things • The Sound of Music • and more.

00290389........................$12.95

GRADING
LI = Lower Intermediate
I = Intermediate
UI = Upper Intermediate

FOR MORE INFORMATION, SEE YOUR LOCAL MUSIC DEALER, OR WRITE TO:

HAL•LEONARD® CORPORATION

7777 W. BLUEMOUND RD. P.O. BOX 13819 MILWAUKEE, WI 53213

www.halleonard.com